# Meerkat Mazes

## Hours of meerkat mayhem!

**ARCTURUS**

This edition published in 2012 by Arcturus Publishing Limited
26/27 Bickels Yard, 151–153 Bermondsey Street,
London SE1 3HA

ISBN: 978-1-84858-857-8
CH002452EN
Supplier 16, Date 0812, Print Run 1886

Edited by Kate Overy and Samantha Noonan
Design and illustration by Dynamo Limited

Printed in Singapore

# Contents

# Meet the Meerkat family

Get ready to meet the most adventurous family in the world – the Meerkat family! These crazy critters live in a huge underground burrow in Meerkatville, but they can pop up anywhere on earth, at any time!

## Mr Meerkat

Mr Meerkat used to be in the Meerkat Guards, defending the burrows from snakes. He loves to go on adventures with his family.

## Mrs Meerkat

Mrs Meerkat is an artist and she loves beautiful things. Everywhere she goes, she likes to pick up a pretty souvenir to remind her of the place when she's at home.

## Grandad Morris Meerkat

Morris Meerkat is a great inventor. His finest invention to date is his super Meerkat Time Machine!

## Matt Meerkat

Matt Meerkat loves to play sports and games! He has bags of energy and is always trying to make his family play with him.

## Aunty Myrtle Meerkat

Myrtle Meerkat likes a good gossip and loves to play with her niece and nephews. She is always trying out new clothes and hairstyles.

## Mickey Meerkat

Mickey Meerkat loves to explore. He is always scampering off to investigate things and often gets left behind.

## Milly Meerkat

Milly Meerkat is a fearless meerkat. There is no activity too extreme or scary for her, but her parents won't let her do a lot of them until she is older!

# Meerkats At Home

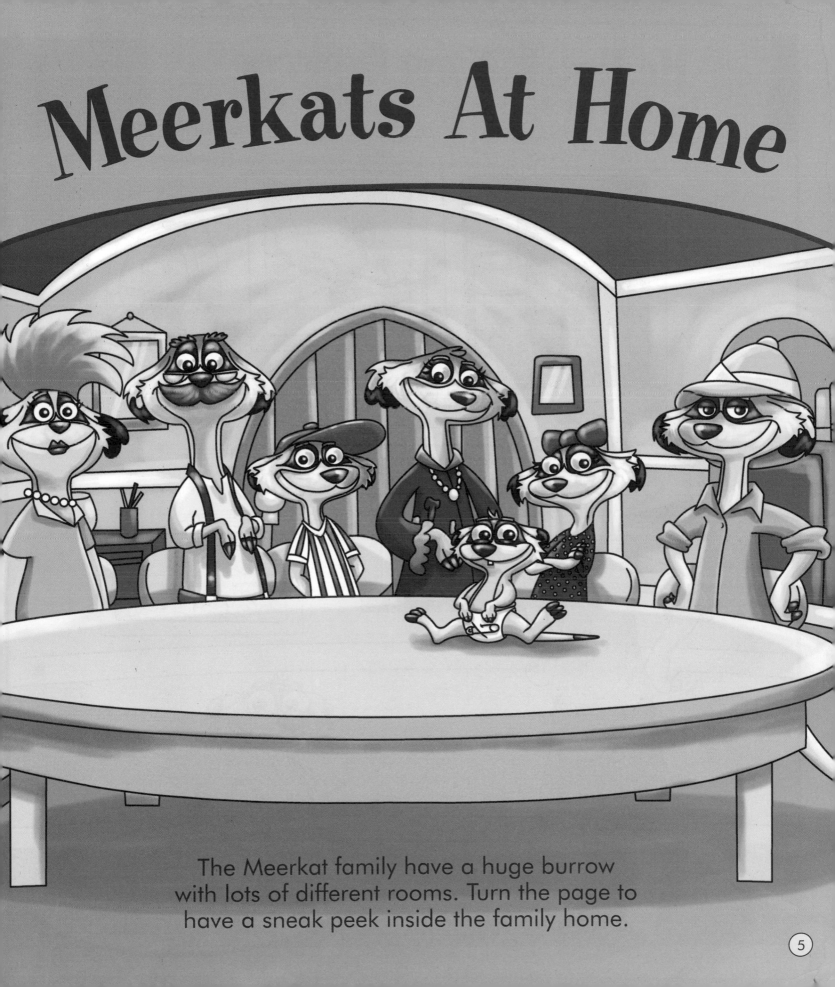

The Meerkat family have a huge burrow
with lots of different rooms. Turn the page to
have a sneak peek inside the family home.

# Mr Meerkat the Explorer

Mr Meerkat likes to take his family on lots of adventures to prepare them for life as adult meerkats.

Mr Meerkat keeps all his adventure equipment in the cellar. Can you help him find his favourite green bag?

Start

Finish

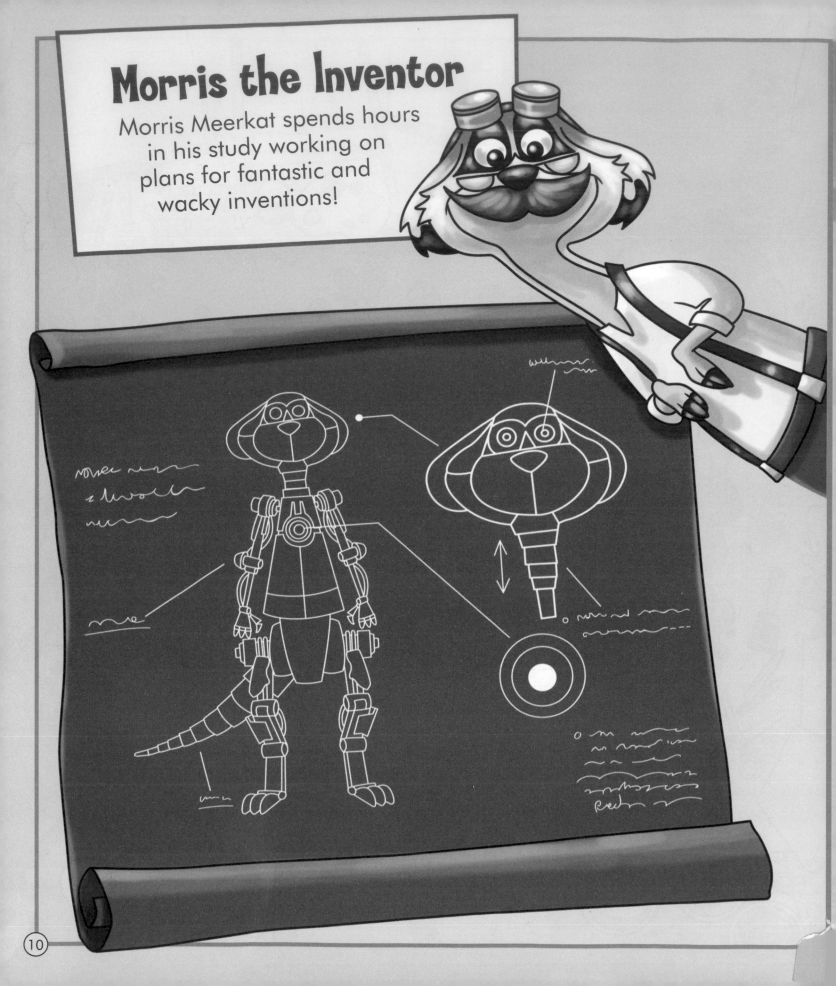

# Morris the Inventor

Morris Meerkat spends hours in his study working on plans for fantastic and wacky inventions!

Morris has lost his latest blueprint. Guide him through his study to find it.

Start

Finish

11

# Matt and Milly's Lost Wheels

Matt and Milly are at the Meerkatville sports field for the afternoon. Unfortunately they have lost some of their kit.

a  b  c

d  e

Can you follow the lines and work out which leads to Matt's skateboard and Milly's missing rollerblade?

14

# Off To See The World!

The family are ready to set off on a new adventure.

Can you spot eight differences between these pictures of them leaving their burrow?

# Mr Meerkat's Adventures

Mr Meerkat thinks expeditions are fun, so he is taking his family out to experience lots of different kinds of adventure.

# Escape the Snakes!

The snakes are the sworn enemies of the meerkats. Mr Meerkat is a skilled fighter and keeps his family safe when they are travelling in the underground tunnels.

a

b

c

d

e

f

g

h

i

j

Can you spot two sneaky snakes that are exactly the same?

Oh no, Mickey has wandered off into the snake infested tunnels! Guide Mr Meerkat through the maze to save him.
Start
Finish

Milly stopped to look at a lion and now she's been left behind! Help her hurry along the game trails to find Mrs Meerkat.

Start

Finish

Mrs Meerkat really wants to buy a pink and green carpet. Can you lead her through the market to find one?
Start
Finish

Oh no! Mickey has knocked over one of the experiments! Help the family get out of the lab quickly.

Start

Finish

# Paint Peril!

Paintballing is a way for all the family to have fun! It's fast, exciting and messy – a perfect adventure!

Follow the tangle lines to see who just shot Milly!

Morris Meerkat is tired and needs a little sit down, but to get to the rest area, he needs to navigate through the battle! Can you help him?

Start

Finish

# Meerkat Knights

Next stop, medieval England to see the meerkat knights of old competing in a tournament.

```
T T F N Z J L A P K Q
V G B C W L A R B N C
C B A Z I I N M N I A
D Q N U A O C O Q G N
F Z N H N E E U F H I
U O E N M T N R A T U
H S R D H E L M E T D
O W U H S H I E L D J
R O D Y K A U Z T G C
S R B E X N J O U S T
E D G X S U R N V D O
```

KNIGHT     JOUST
ARMOUR     LANCE
SWORD     HORSE
SHIELD     GAUNTLET
HELMET     BANNER

Can you find these words in the grid above?

# Be Prepared

Mr Meerkat believes you should always be ready for adventure!

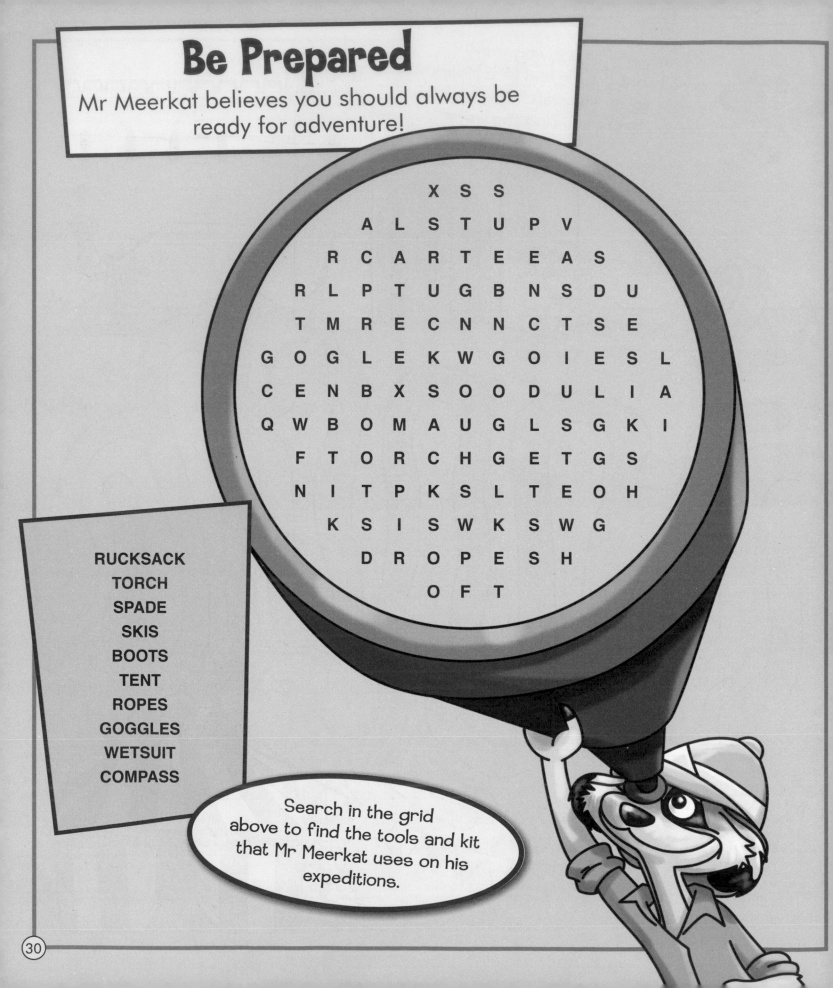

```
        X S S
      A L S T U P V
      R C A R T E E A S
      R L P T U G B N S D U
      T M R E C N N C T S E
    G O G L E K W G O I E S L
    C E N B X S O O D U L I A
    Q W B O M A U G L S G K I
    F T O R C H G E T G S
    N I T P K S L T E O H
      K S I S W K S W G
        D R O P E S H
          O F T
```

**RUCKSACK**
**TORCH**
**SPADE**
**SKIS**
**BOOTS**
**TENT**
**ROPES**
**GOGGLES**
**WETSUIT**
**COMPASS**

Search in the grid above to find the tools and kit that Mr Meerkat uses on his expeditions.

# Matt and Milly's Thrill-seeking Trip

Matt and Milly live for sports and games. They love to travel the world to find the most exciting things to do!

# Aloha Hawaii

The Meerkat family have come to Hawaii, for some sun, sea and sand.

# Moon Landing

The Moon has many secrets and Morris Meerkat is determined to explore them all!

a

b

c

d

e

Can you spot which of these Cheese People is the odd one out?

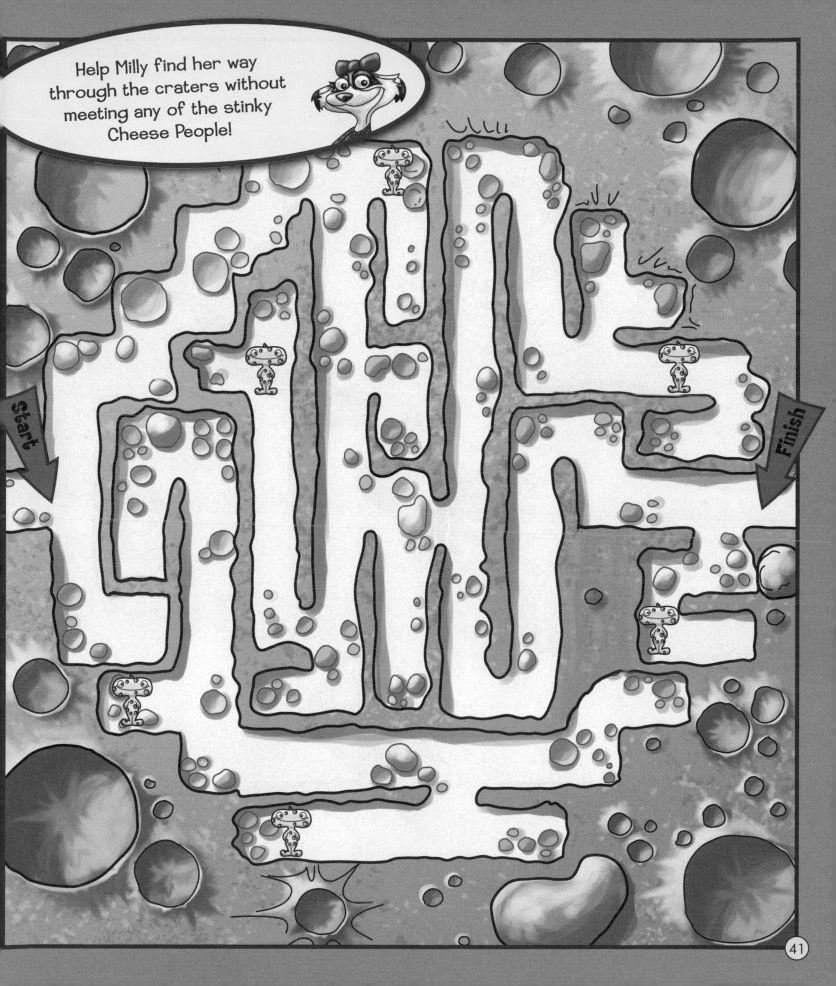

# Roll Up, Roll Up!

The Meerkat family love going to the circus – and joining in!

Can you spot six differences between these two meerkat cannonballs?

Matt wants to ask the clown to teach him how to juggle. Help him find his way across the circus ring.

Start

Finish

# Family Fun

The Meerkats have popped up somewhere new!
Who knows what the adventure will be this time!

Look carefully at these two pictures of them popping up and see if you can spot seven differences.

# Morris Meerkat's
# Time Machine

Morris is very proud of his time machine. It is his best invention and he loves to use it to take the family out.

# Roman Roads

Morris has brought the family back to the dangerous days of the Roman Empire.

Unfortunately he's made a bit of a mess of the statues. Can you match each statue to the correct shadow?

# Napoleonic Wars

Morris Meerkat has brought the family back to a time of great sea battles during the Napoleonic wars.

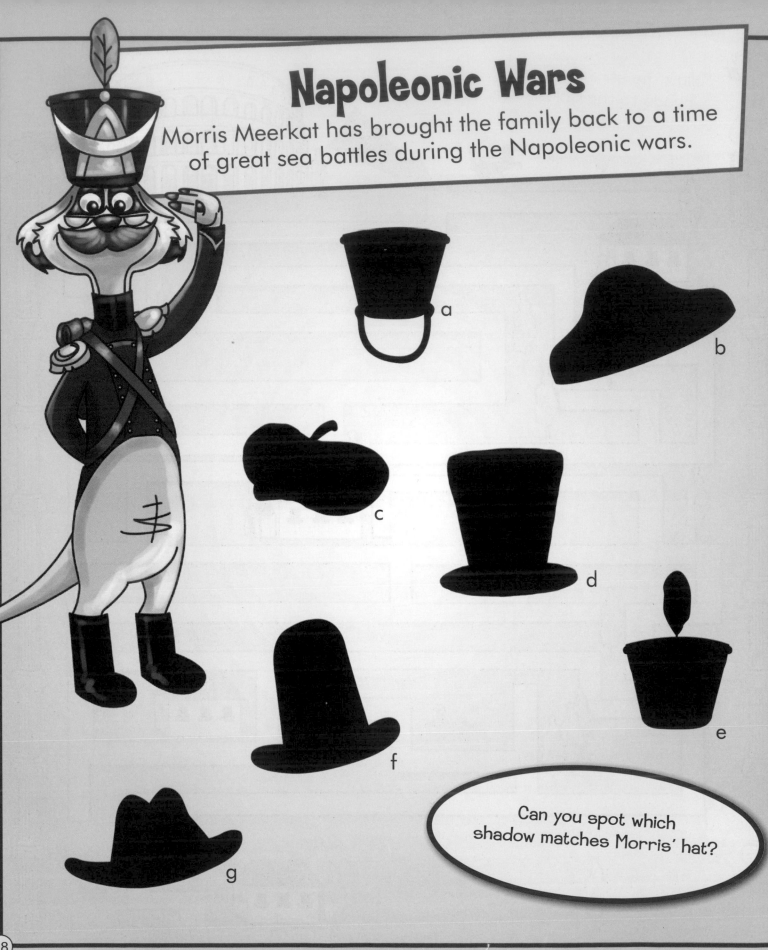

Can you spot which shadow matches Morris' hat?

Guide Milly through the terracotta meerkat army to look at the special Ming vase.

Start

Finish

51

# Run Like An Egyptian!

Mickey has asked his Grandad if they can go back to Ancient Egypt – he wants to find a mummy!

Can you decipher the stone tablet Mickey has found in a nearby pyramid?

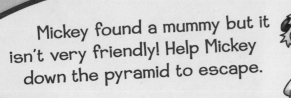

Mickey found a mummy but it isn't very friendly! Help Mickey down the pyramid to escape.

The family have had a lovely day visiting an alien city, but it's time to go home. Can you guide Morris and Milly have through the city to meet the others?
Finish
Start

# Diary Entry

Morris has had a lovely day with his family, but his memory isn't what it was.

We had a very _____ day today. In the morning we went to ___ to have a look around. The soldiers were a bit stern! Then, we went back to the Napoleonic _____ to see the old _____ in action, which the children loved. Next, we travelled back to ancient ___ and Milly had fun with the terracotta ___. Then we had a quick visit to the _____. A few too many ___ for my taste! I thought it would be nice to finish with a _____ adventure to teach the children about the dinosaurs, but it went a bit wrong! Very tired now, time for ___ !

**ARMY**
**BED**
**CHINA**
**EXCITING**
**FUTURE**
**SHIPS**
**PREHISTORIC**
**WARS**
**ROBOTS**
**ROME**

Can you help him finish his diary entry?

# Myrtle Meerkat's
# Busy Day

Myrtle Meerkat is always busy
shopping, cooking or taking
her nephews and niece
out on trips.

# Fabulous Fashion!

The next stop is the Meerkat fashion show! Myrtle loves all the different fabrics and colours.

Milly was having such fun backstage, she didn't notice the rest of the family were leaving! Help her through all the clothes to catch up.

Start

Finish

Mickey really wants to have some cherry pie but he can't reach it from his seat. Help him scurry across the table before his mother can catch him!

Start

Finish

# Splashing Fun

All the family love going to the gym.
Whilst Myrtle enjoys her workout, the
rest of the family swim.

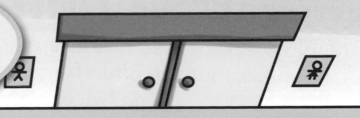

Mr Meerkat is going to have one last dive and then get out. Can you guide him to the diving board and then the steps?

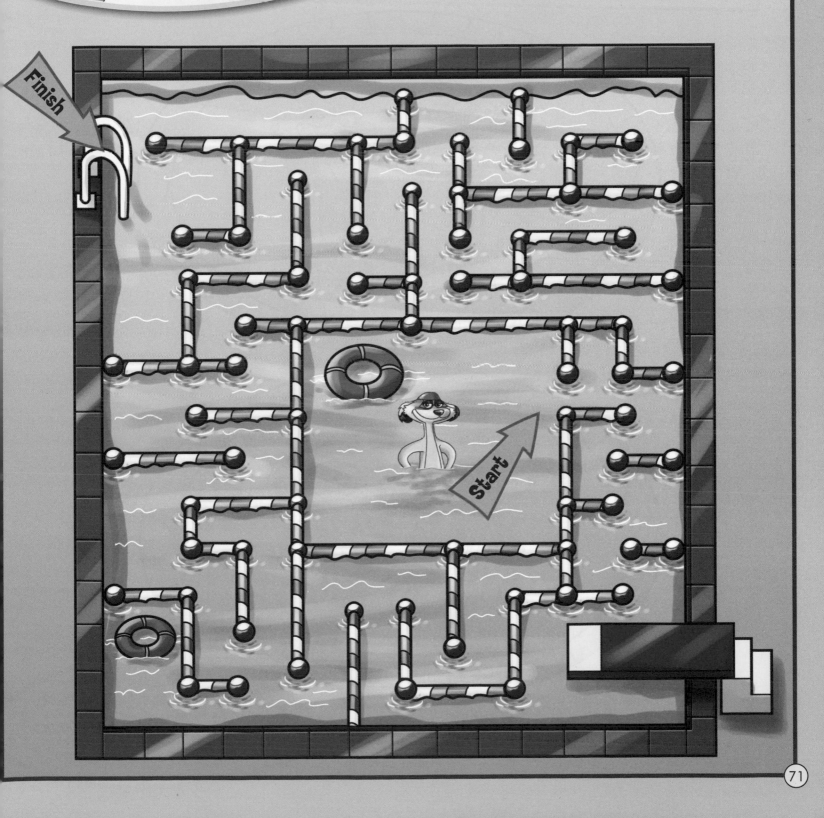

# Proud Aunty

Myrtle Meerkat is so proud of her niece and nephews that she often frames the same photo twice!

Can you spot six differences between these prints of her latest picture?

# Meerkats on Holiday

The Meerkat family are off on a tropical holiday today!

Milly was watching the planes take off outside and has been left behind. Guide her through the airport.

Start

Finish

# Fancy Grub

On their first evening on holiday, the meerkats go to a posh restaurant as a treat!

Oh no! Grandad Morris can't find his way back to the table! Can you guide him through the restaurant?

# Meerkats Have Talent!

The Meerkat family's favourite show, Meerkats Have Talent is being filmed in the resort they are staying at so they sit in the audience to watch Morris take part in the show.

Milly would love to meet her favourite judge, Miranda Brightclaws, but she needs to find a way through to her dressing room first!

Start

Finish

# Burrow, Sweet Burrow

The family are sad to end their fantastic holiday, but they do enjoy being back home.

Myrtle is struggling with her heavy suitcase and has fallen behind the rest of the family. Help her through the tunnels to the front door.

Finish

Start

# Party Time!

Today is Mickey's birthday so the family are celebrating.

# Present Jumble

Mickey wants to open his present from Matt first. Can you help him find it?

1. It is tied with a blue ribbon.
2. It has red wrapping paper.
3. The paper has more than three spots.

# Answers

# MEERKATS AT HOME

### Page 6-7 Mr Meerkat the Explorer

Mr Meerkat's favourite adventure was in cold, snowy Canada, shown in picture d

### Page 8-9 Mrs Meerkat's Paint Puzzle

### Page 10-11 Morris the Inventor

### Page 12-13 Aunty Myrtle's Treats

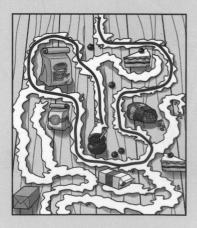

# Answers

## Page 14-15 Matt and Milly's Lost Wheels
Matt's skateboard is on line b
Milly's rollerblade is on line d

## Page 16 Off To See The World!

# MR MEERKAT'S ADVENTURES

## Page 18-19 Escape the Snakes!
Snakes d and i are exactly the same

## Page 20-21 Sunny Safari
Mr Meerkat's favourite green bag is on line c

## Page 22-23 Market in Morrocco
Carpet d is the odd one out

## Page 24-25 Messy Meerkats
Tap a empties into beaker 3
Tap b empties into beaker 1
Tap c empties into beaker 2

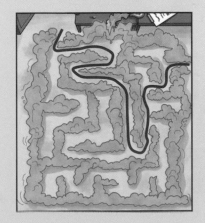

# Answers

## Page 26-27  Paint Peril!
Matt shot Milly with his paintball gun

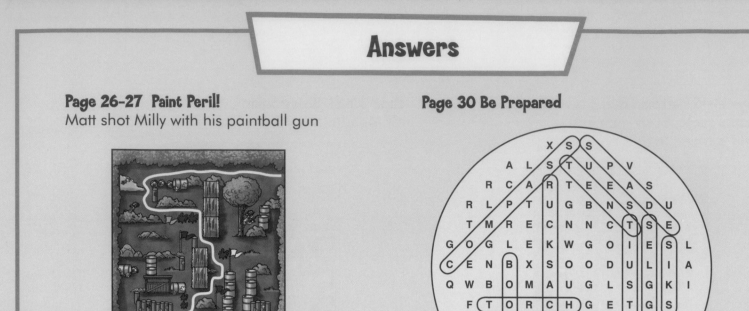

## Page 28-29  Meerkat Knights

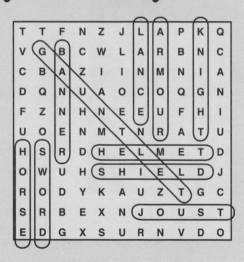

## Page 30 Be Prepared

# MATT AND MILLY'S
# THRILL-SEEKING TRIP

## Page 32-33  Speedy Skiing
Matt's snow gear pieces are b, c and f
Myrtle's snow gear pieces are a, d and e

# Answers

## P34-35  Ninja Meerkats
Milly needs to use rope a to climb to the roof

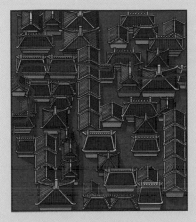

## Page 37  Shiver Me Timbers

## Page 39  Aloha Hawaii

## Page 40-41  Moon Landing
Cheese Person c is the odd one out

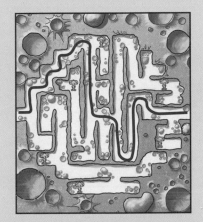

## Page 42-43  Roll Up, Roll Up!

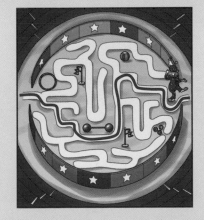

# Answers

## Page 44 Family Fun

## MORRiS MEERKAT'S TiME MACHiNE

### Page 46-47 Roman Roads

Statue a matches shadow 2, statue b matches shadow 3, statue c matches shadow 1, statue d matches shadow 4

### Page 48-49 Napoleonic Wars

Shadow e matches Morris' hat

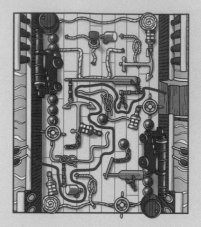

### Page 50-51 The Ming Dynasty

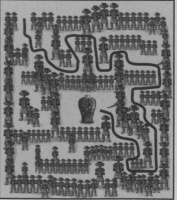

# Answers

## Page 52-53 Run Like An Egyptian!
The message reads:
THE SECRET ENTRANCE IS BY THE SPHINX

## Page 56-57 Prehistoric World
Footprint a matches footprint h, footprint b matches footprint g, footprint c matches footprint d, footprint e matches footprint f

## Page 54-55 To The Future!

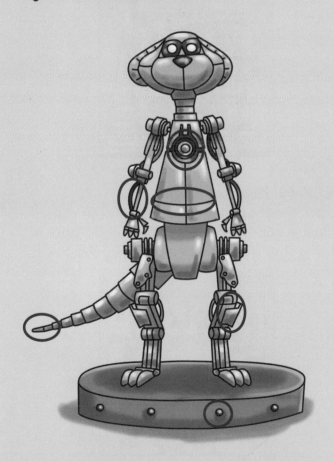

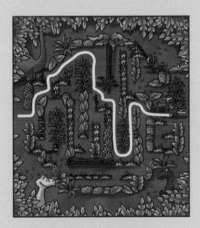

## Page 58 Diary Entry
We had a very <u>exciting</u> day today. In the morning we went to <u>Rome</u> to have a look around. The soldiers were a bit stern! Then, we went back to the Napoleonic <u>wars</u> to see the old <u>ships</u> in action, which the children loved. Next, we travelled back to ancient <u>China</u> and Milly had fun with the terracotta <u>army</u>. Then we had a quick visit to the <u>future</u>. A few too many <u>robots</u> for my taste! I thought it would be nice to finish with a <u>prehistoric</u> adventure to teach the children about the dinosaurs, but it went a bit wrong! Very tired now, time for <u>bed</u>!

# Answers

## MYRTLE MEERKAT'S BUSY DAY

### Page 60-61 Beauty Salon
Mrs Meerkat's hairdryer goes to lead c

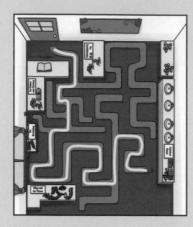

### Page 62-63  Mount Olympus
Shadow d matches the statue

### Page 65 Fabulous Fashion

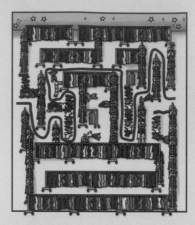

### Page 67 A Fine Feast

### Page 68-69  Playgroup Puzzle
Robot 1 matches shadow c, robot 2 matches shadow e, robot 3 matches shadow d, robot 4 matches shadow a, robot 5 matches shadow b

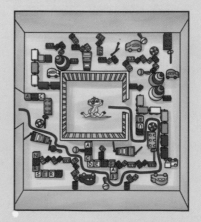

# Answers

## Page 71 Splashing Fun

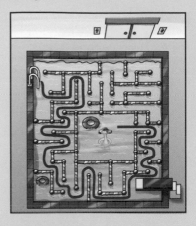

## Page 72 Proud Aunty

## MEERKATS ON HOLIDAY

### Page 74-75 Up, Up And Away!

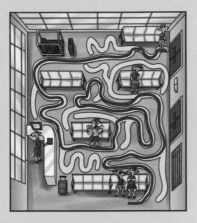

## Page 76-77 Under The Sea
Line b leads to the starfish

## Page 79 Fancy Grub

# Answers

## Page 81 Meerkats Have Talent

## Page 83 Burrow, Sweet Burrow

## Page 85 Party Time

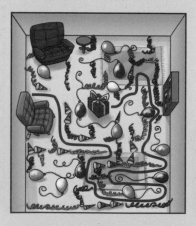

### Page 86 Present Jumble
The present from Matt is a